CUTTING YOUR CAR USE

Cutting Your Car Use

Save Money, Be Healthy, Be Green!

ANNA SEMLYEN

Illustrated by Axel Scheffler

Green Books

This colour edition first published in 2007
by Green Books Ltd
Foxhole, Dartington, Totnes, Devon TQ9 6EB
edit@greenbooks.co.uk www.greenbooks.co.uk

Text printed by Cambrian Printers, Aberystwyth, UK
on Cyclus Offset paper (100% post-consumer waste)

ISBN 978 1 900322 15 7

DISCLAIMER: The advice in this book is believed to be correct at the time of printing, but readers should seek expert or professional advice if in doubt about any of the recommendations made.

If you would like to discuss a possible bulk purchase of this book, please phone Green Books on 01803 863260.

Contents

Acknowledgements

I am extremely grateful to the following: Judy Ballard, Ali Clabburn, Richard Evans, David Henshaw, Anthea Nicholson, Valerie Belsey, and Amanda Cuthbert and John Elford of Green Books.

My thanks go to Randall Ghent for adapting this book for North America. Some of his references are in this edition.

The map of the National Cycle Network is from Sustrans. The extract from the Safer Routes to Schools map on page 19 was drawn by Philip Griffin, and is reproduced courtesy of Radstock Primary School, Earley Town Council, Wokingham District Council and the Pedestrians Association (now Living Streets).

Introduction

Imagine a land where every child can walk or cycle to school in safety, where local shops thrive and a car is not essential to enjoy life. Picture how different your neighbourhood would be with fewer moving cars. How much better would your life be if you were in a car less often? Petrol supplies will soon be declining and energy prices are likely to rise sharply. Cutting your car use will save you money, improve your health and improve everyone's quality of life.

This book gives practical advice on reducing traffic by changing personal habits. If you are:

• A car driver

• Wanting to limit your driving, save money, be healthier and greener

• Thinking of sharing or selling a car

• Teaching or studying environmental or transport issues

then this book is for you.

Many people think that there is too much car traffic. There is a lot that you can do to tackle car dependency. YOU CAN MAKE A DIFFERENCE. This book shows you how.

Throughout this book, helpful organisations in **bold print** are listed in the directory at the back. For local information – for instance local car sharing – see the transport and travel pages of your council's website.

Chapter 1

Why cut your car use?

Cars are useful in some situations and essential in others, but need not be used for 63% of all journeys. Successful traffic reduction involves cutting unnecessary trips, choosing local shops and facilities, more walking and cycling, together with car sharing and use of public transport. Even if you could not manage without a car, or do not want a car-free lifestyle, there are many incentives for driving less, both financial and for a better quality of life.

British households spend £1 in every £7 on motoring.

To save money

Are you driving to work, or working to drive? Use the tables below to work out savings from not driving. Alternatively, **www.eta.co.uk/tools/carcalcstart.asp** has a web calculator, and at **www.carplus.org.uk** under 'Costs and benefits of car clubs' you can download an Excel spreadsheet, or get one from **www.cuttingyourcaruse.co.uk**.

	From	To	Miles	Fuel Cost	Time	Alternative	Cost	Time
Mon								
Tue								
Wed								
Thu								
Fri								
Sat								
Sun								
TOTAL								

Estimate your total car costs using the chart below:

	£
Car purchase (including interest on a loan) and depreciation	
Insurance	
VED (road tax)	
MOT, servicing, spares and repairs	
Breakdown service	
Fuel	
Parking and garaging	
Fines and congestion charges	
Total per year £	

> *If you drive a small second-hand car 5,000 miles a year, it will cost around £2,800, i.e. £7.50 per day or 56p a mile; or £3,480 a year for a new Vauxhall Corsa doing 6,000 miles per year. A bike, including purchase, depreciation, insurance, servicing, spares and weatherproof clothing, will cost under £200 a year.*

Congestion and motorway charging are likely to become widespread. Holland has agreed to a national scheme. London's £8 a day congestion charge has reduced traffic by 20%.

Is your car worth the money it costs and the time it takes to earn it? Plus the time in car care? The typical British driver devotes three and a half hours of every 16 waking hours to their car. There are cheaper options:

- Walk: cheapest and healthiest of all

- Phone, text, internet, teleconferencing and videoconferencing, or get things delivered: saves car costs and time

- Cycle: cycling costs very little. Folding bikes can link to a lift, train, bus or taxi

- Lift share: sharing fuel costs (around 13p a mile – 7p each) is usual

- Bus: a day or weekly pass can save you money

- Train: get a weekly or monthly pass using discount cards. Book in advance and on line for special offers

Why cut your car use?

- Car Hire: ask car hire firms, or join a car club

- Taxi: cheaper if you only use your car occasionally

With one car less, you could use taxis or car hire when necessary and you could try out different models of car.

> *If you drive under 8,000 miles a year, being car-free could save you money.*

To add up your total travel costs and compare the alternatives see **www.carclubs.org.uk** – a spreadsheet programme does the maths for you. Send a SAE for a free paper copy to **Semlyen**. At **www.citycarclub.co.uk/calculator.php** there is a savings calculator for membership of a car club. The **AA** also have a free motoring costs leaflet.

SUCCESS STORY

DH last owned an 'inherited' car for six months in 1996. He has cut his driving steadily from around 5,000 miles p.a. Now he rarely hires, and has adapted his lifestyle to do almost all he needs on a bike, bus or train. He advises others to plan, "and then realise how much money, time and other resources you save – but most of all be thorough in the understanding of your other possible travel modes." Since selling his car, DH has raised his quality of life, saved "loads of dosh" and reduced his blood pressure and pulse rate. His weight is consistent, he is almost always knows how long a journey across town will take, and can shop in under an hour at any time of day.

To be healthy

Air Quality

> *On average bus users face a third less pollution than car users.*

- In-car air can be three times as toxic as air breathed by cyclists or walkers, because cars travel in the middle of the road, where pollution is most concentrated

- Exhaust fumes are poisons: and with one in seven children suffering from asthma, more people dying prematurely from road pollution than are killed in crashes, less traffic is better for everyone's lungs

Exercise

> *Regularly walking or cycling reduces risks of coronary heart disease by up to 50% and stroke by 66%.*

Now for the good news!

- Walking is better than low salt diets for lowering blood pressure. It also increases bone mass and reduces fat

- Cycling five miles, four times a week, can cut risks of coronary heart disease by up to half

- In a trial, non-exercisers who began cycling around 19 miles a week rapidly improved their aerobic fitness by over 11%. Cycling can also significantly reduce body fat

- Walking and cycling often give you the chance to use back roads and paths, reducing your exposure to traffic noise and fumes

To be green

Road transport is the fastest growing source of greenhouse gas emissions, which cause climate change. By driving less you can help fight the trend of global warming and natural disasters and help to preserve fast-dwindling oil reserves.

> *Road transport is responsible for 22% of the UK's total greenhouse gas emissions.*

SUCCESS STORY

Marcus Jones lives near his transport consultancy work, to which he commutes by bicycle. Didcot has a station and he is within walking distance of shops and public transport. Marcus and his wife sold their car as they didn't like driving or wasting money and believe that unnecessary car use is socially irresponsible. They bought good luggage-carrying equipment for their bikes and a shopping trolley. On rare occasions when a car is needed they hire the right vehicle for the job. Marcus advises others to "add up the true costs of driving before choosing to live far away from work". As a non-car owner he enjoys savings and greater freedom.

To manage time

Are you really saving time by driving?

- Could you cut your 'taxi' duty by giving your children public transport passes or by arranging a lift share?
- Could you telework at home, or work while you travel on a train?

MAKE A START Begin by experimenting with travelling less or using alternatives.

Charities: **Campaign for Better Transport, Sustrans, Living Streets** and **Friends of the Earth**. Helplines include **Energy Saving Trust, Air Pollution Enquiries** and **NHS Direct**.

Chapter 2

How are you using your car?

Start by analysing how and why you travel. 'Location, location, location' is a catchphrase for house purchase and applies to all activities when cutting car use. Aim to reduce your need to travel.

- Ask your council or employer for Individualised Travel Marketing, where an transport expert analyses your travel and suggests changes. It reduces car trips by up to 13%.

Commuting

- If possible, choose work by its proximity to your home or choose to live near good public transport links

- Try either walking, cycling, public transport or sharing a lift. The best journey planning site is **www.transportdirect.info**

- Ask to work shifts with people with whom you could lift share. See **www.liftshare.com**

- Request flexi-time. Employers are required by law to consider flexi-time requests by parents with children under 6 years.

- Ask for compressed working (when you can take a day off if hours are worked in advance). There was a 16% cut in sick leave after its introduction in Irvine in California. Working a nine-day fortnight means a 10% reduction in commuting

- If possible, work at home. (The Royal Bank of Scotland allows employees to work from home on a voluntary basis, and cuts travel and subsistence by teleconferencing)

- Consider part-time work. Being car-free may save a day's net wages weekly

- Talk to your manager about workplace travel plans (see below)

Information is available from **Campaign for Better Transport** and the **Telework Association**.

For workplace travel plans see the **Energy Saving Trust** and the **DfT**'s free guides, and Chapter 8. Business advice is available from **Energy Saving Trust**, **Association for Commuter Transport** and **Campaign for Better Transport**.

> *17% of car trips are for travelling to and from work.*

Business journeys

You generally have less choice over business travel than over commuting. Ask about:

- Company travel policy – is there a workplace travel plan?

- Details of lump sum and/or mileage allowances for car/bicycle/walking, passenger mileages and a car pool or car club

- Refunds for delivery services, public transport, taxi fares or discount travel passes, phone use /business phone cards

- Availability of a car sharing system, including priority parking (which guarantees a taxi home if car sharing fails), pool cars, car clubs or folding bicycles

- **Booost** and **CycleScheme** administer ways of employees getting up to 50% off new bikes and equipment by paying monthly via salary reductions. This saves the employer and employee tax.

For urban journeys, cycling beats a car in peak hours and is quicker than a bus for journeys up to 8 miles.

School journeys

School journeys are the first journeys of the day and affect children's health and future travel habits. In term-time about 20% of morning rush hour traffic is taken up by the school run.

Travel Awareness

- Choose your nearest school and consider re-locating or working nearer if necessary
- Teach children road and personal safety
- Choose a quiet route if possible and walk or cycle together
- Familiarise your children with local public transport, timetables and independent travel
- Make children aware of the locations of hazards on their normal route(s) – e.g. crossing busy roads
- You could put up local walking, cycling and public transport maps at home

Work with your child's school

Schools can take many initiatives to cut school traffic and make it safer for walkers and cyclists:

- Include a safer routes map in the prospectus
- Organise an escort scheme. A 'Walking or Cycling Bus' entails an adult collecting children along a pre-arranged route
- Run/endorse a lift share scheme
- Review the visibility of uniforms and give out reflectives
- Request slower speed limits on approach roads (20 mph)

How are you using your car?

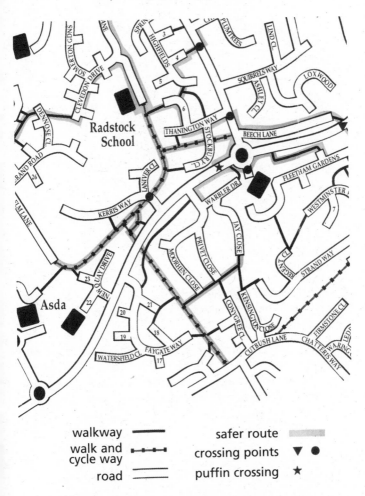

**An example of a safer route to school map,
available from Living Streets**

CUTTING YOUR CAR USE

- Create safe crossings, e.g. with crossing patrols. Some schools designate dropping-off points to avoid congestion.

- Have car-free entrances

- Hold cars back until pedestrians and cyclists have left school

- Have secure and visible cycle shelters

- Have lockers/storage for books, cycling gear and outdoor clothing

- Do a homework review to reduce the amount carried

- Use 'safe routes' as a class topic

- Put up a school journey notice board with maps, timetables, car share

- Explore options for new services e.g. better routes and low fares linked to a code of behaviour for school bus users

A free copy of *A Safer Journey to School: A guide to school travel plans for parents, teachers and governors* is available from the **DCSF**. **Sustrans** offers free information about **Safe Routes to Schools**. See **Hedgehogs** and **Arrive Alive** road safety sites.

SUCCESS STORY

Project manager MB from Oxford drastically cut her car use from 12,000 to 4,000 miles p.a. because of cost, the environment and fitness. She 'commuter ride shares' with four others. Although work involves a 30 mile round trip, she deliberately chose city living, near bus routes and local shops. She drives to a supermarket just once a fortnight, and takes a bus to the station even though her job will pay for a taxi. MB books cheap rail tickets and works on the train – an effective use of company time. Her advice is to cycle. "It's just a habit, gets you fit, is sometimes quicker – you just need the right clothing and accessories." MB could not sell her car – there are no public services to work and she shares the drive. But she saves over £600 p.a. in fuel plus £100 in servicing and spares even after transport fares.

Shopping journeys

24% of car trips in Britain are shopping trips. To reduce these you could:

- Walk or cycle to local food shops
- Share a car or taxi with neighbours, and benefit from 'two for the price of one' offers. Fix a weekly day and time
- Take a taxi to bulk buy
- Consider making or growing more food yourself

Home Deliveries

> *Home delivery for a market town catchment can save around 70-80% of the driving distance.*

- Most major supermarkets and some local stores offer delivery services, either through on line ordering or by telephone or fax. Some will pack a hand-written list

- See if any local shops deliver

- Farms/ box schemes. By buying direct from farms you'll get the best seasonal produce. Ask the **Soil Association** about Local Food Links which help consumers buy through vegetable box schemes, food co-ops and farmers' markets

Social journeys

Try to plan your social activities with minimal use of a car.

- Include a map and travel information with alternatives to the car on your invitations, or suggest meeting up at public transport interchanges

- Walking and cycling provide more opportunities to meet and talk to people than driving

- Make local contacts by walking or cycling to local shops and amenities

---

── SUCCESS STORY ──

Adrian Lane, a civil servant from Sheffield, sold his car. He says: "We should be prepared to work harder at making the alternatives work – researching timetables, cycling, walking etc.. Remember why you are doing it. For me it was because of information on the consequences of car use, and for health, environmental and cost reasons." Adrian says he is healthier, fitter and happier. His urban journey times are generally shorter, he has more energy, plus new friends and knowledge about the environment and transport issues generally.

Leisure journeys

Country trips are often a reason given for car ownership, but many towns, villages, tourist attractions and leisure activities can be reached by public transport.

- Find local leisure pursuits – explore from your door. Use the **Sustrans** National Cycle Network or the **National Byway**. Ideally, choose hobbies that are reachable by public transport

- Look up the attraction's website for maps and travel details by sustainable transport

---

── SUCCESS STORY ──

Jo Rathbone from Earlsdon, Coventry, cut her mileage from 915 to 355 miles per month by sharing a car with another family. They each have it on alternate weekends, with other time negotiated. "Not having a car instantly available is the best way of not using it, especially for short journeys." For Jo, finance was the main reason for driving less, plus green issues. She was happy to not to own a car, but her husband wanted to. "When we heard neighbours were considering buying one and didn't really want to, we teamed up. Sharing works very well." They now shop locally and are more active in the community. "We are more dependent on others for lifts, which builds relation-ships." Jo cycles and walks more, which raises her fitness. "The children love travelling by train and bus and are understanding that we can't always do everything. Hobbies must be in walking/busing distance."

Chapter 3

Looking at the alternatives

Walking

- Is cheap – you just need comfort-able shoes and a map

- Is healthy – as well as improving fit-ness, it exposes you to one third of the fumes of car travel

- Gives you the opportunity to meet people en route

Charities include **Living Streets**, **Sustrans** and the **Ramblers Association** for leisure. **Transport for London** have walking maps and some council's Rights of Way departments may offer advice on routes and access. Investigate local contacts for volunteer-led walks: ask your library about 'Walking The Way to Health'.

Lift sharing

Most of us share cars regularly, with friends and family, without thinking about it. But there are times when dri-vers have empty seats because they don't know anyone who needs a lift. Organised lift-sharing is a solution.

CUTTING YOUR CAR USE

- Register with the Liftshare 08700 11 11 99 or at **www.lift-share.com** (the UK's largest), or try **www.carshare.com**, **www.nationalcarshare.co.uk**, **www.shareajourney.com**. You'll automatically be matched with someone to share the journey and its costs. There are many local websites – see your local council website

- Park & share sites: this is when people travel independently to a meeting point and then share a car to a common destination, e.g. to a town from a secure car park on a ring road

Lift-sharing benefits you, the community and the environment. It reduces travel costs, lessens congestion, pollution, parking problems, the need for a private car, and is a solution to public transport problems. It is also a way to meet like-minded people.

At £1 per litre, the average cost of fuel is 13p a mile. If each passenger pays the driver 7p per mile, then giving one person a lift halves the driver's fuel costs and giving two people a lift entirely covers the fuel cost.

Before sharing, think about your safety:

- Avoid exchanging home addresses with your travelling companions before you meet them

If half of UK motorists received a lift one day a week, pollution would be reduced by 10% and traffic jams by 20%.

Looking at the alternatives

- Arrange to meet in a public place

- Arrange to meet near public transport links, so you have an alternative means of travelling should the lift fall through

- Tell a friend or family member when and where you are travelling, and with whom

- The first time you lift share with a stranger, satisfy yourself as to his or her identity. You could ask for an ID, such as passport, student card or driving licence

---

——— SUCCESS STORY ———

Swindon housewife Ruth Chivers drives 50% less to get fit, save money, reduce pollution and be an example to her children. She organises her time so that walking, cycling or using public transport are real choices, rather than driving "in a last minute rush". Doing a few jobs in one round trip makes journeys more productive. Ruth shares lifts with other parents, and talks about car use with her family of four so that it is not taken for granted. "Whatever the weather it is always possible to wrap up warm or wear waterproofs. My daughter has enjoyed the two mile walk to kindergarten since the age of three. Walking, cycling or using public transport is quality time – an opportunity for the family to talk and enjoy the changing seasons. Plus it is quicker and less hassle to cycle to town than drive and park."

Taxis

Taxis provide a 24-hour, chauffeur-driven car at your door with very little notice. They are convenient and cut parking time and worries about directions. Journey times are quicker in areas where taxis can use bus lanes, and a taxi is safer if you plan to drink.

- Taxis cost less than car hire for around the first 30 miles, though car clubs are cheaper
- To cut costs even further, organise a regular taxi share e.g. to town from a village to buy food

www.traintaxi.co.uk can be used to find out the phone numbers of taxis serving most stations in England.

Virgin trains run a Carlink scheme to book a taxi to or from a rail station. Or phone **National Cabline** if your don't know a local firm. **Transport for All** support disabled travellers in London.

> *For the cost of running a car, you could spend £8 per day on taxis.*

Cycling

Modern gears and a lightweight machine make for an easier ride. If you are unsure what to buy you could hire for a while as a way of deciding. The **CTC** website has a hire list and the **Company of Cyclists** run try-out bike shows.

- Cyclists enjoy more reliable journey times than car users

- Cycling is healthy, clean, quiet and of little risk to others

- Folding bikes can fit on a train, underground, bus, coach, taxi or ferry and give you more flexibility than using cycle racks on cars

- Employees and the self-employed can get tax relief of up to 20p per mile on business travel. Employees can get up to 50% discounts on cycling kit through their employer through **BOOST** or **Cyclescheme**.

- Get cycle training and local maps from your Council

For the latest folding bike advice see **www.atob.org.uk** or ask at your cycle shop. **Brompton** is a British make. A tricycle from **Cycles Maximus** has a trailer or passenger seats.

For disability cycling information, try **Bromakin**, **Logic Engineering Concepts** or **London Recumbents**. Contact **London Cycling Campaign** for their all ability cycling guide.

Cycling (at 10–20 mph) can be the fastest way to travel in urban peak hours.

Safety

- A cycle helmet is optional. Protection will vary according to fitting, speed, and other factors. See **www.cyclehelmets.org**. Gloves are also recommended

- Cycle lights must be British Standard 'Kite'-marked. Some LEDS last for hours even with rechargeable batteries, e.g. Nickel-Metal-Hydrides. Dynamos can be used

- Be seen. Use maximum visibility pedals, put reflectors on the bike and wear reflective clothes if possible. Look for puncture-resistant tyres with a reflective strip

- Consider training, e.g. the National Cycling Training Helpline 0870 607 0415. Learn to avoid major roads, difficult junctions or right turns. Use **Sustrans'** National Cycle Network, **CycleCity Guides**, **London Cycling Campaign** maps, or the **National Byway**

- Find out if there is a local 'bike buddy' scheme: ask at your place of work or see **www.bikebudi.com**

- Consider insurance for personal accident, injury and theft, e.g. **CTC**, **Cycleguard**, **London Cycling Campaign** and **CycleAid** lawyers

- **www.bikeforall.net** is a comprehensive cyclists portal

Maintenance

- Keep tyres inflated to the pressure shown on the tyre.

- Check that you can rock the front of the bike by the handlebars with the front brake on without movement of the headset (the bolt your handlebar stem slots into)

- Check that brakes and gears are working efficiently with cables that are not frayed

- Clean and lubricate the chain with synthetic dry lube such as TF2 or Finish Line

- Check chain tension. It should be firm, not sloppy

- Correct saddle height is when, with your heel on the pedal, your leg is almost straight

Secure your bike

- Buy a good lock.
  See **www.whycycle.co.uk/safety-locks.htm**

- Remember to secure any quick release parts, or get them replaced with fixed versions

- Lock your bike to an immovable object

- Buy an 'inconspicuous' model. Larger BMX and mountain bikes are stolen twice as often as other types. Unusual, ladies' or visually unattractive models face less risk

- Note your bike's make, colour and frame number. Adding a bike to household insurance is cheaper than cycle-specific insurance

- Postcode or tag your bike. Dye stamping on the bottom bracket, or UV pen marker kits are available from police stations

- A folding bike kept with you is unlikely to be stolen

- Join **Cycleguard, Bikeregister.com,** the **Nationwide Cycle Registration** or fit an electronic tag, e.g. **Datatag**

- Fit anchor points for short term parking outside your home or in your shed e.g. the Abus Wall Anchor, ring-ended Rawbolts, a wall bar or Sheffield stand

> *Only 8% of thefts involve cracking a D or U lock. Crime Prevention Officers say that if all cyclists used high quality D-Locks (costing £30+), theft could fall by up to 90%.*

Electric bicycles

You can largely overcome hills and headwinds with a power-assisted cycle, either purpose-built or as a power kit addition. Electric bikes are exempt from tax, insurance and MOT. Minimum riding age is 14.

- A friction-drive kit is an easily installed, low cost unit, but is affected by rain

- A purpose-built hub drive is efficient, quiet and reliable

- Friction drives and cheap hubs have a finite life, whilst crank motors, chain-drive motors and quality hubs should last a lifetime

- Chain-driven rear wheel or pedal crankshaft bikes are purpose-built and efficient

- Folders and tricycles are also available

- An electric bicycle will go an average of 15 powered miles at 14 mph before a re-charge

Batteries

Lead-acid gel-cell batteries are cheap, easy to maintain and reliable but output gradually diminishes if not serviced. Nickel Cadmium batteries (NiCds) hold 25% more energy by weight, but cost more and are a disposal hazard. The newer Nickel-Metal-Hydride's are slightly better environmentally.

- See **www.atob.org.uk** for details. The editors of A to B Magazine recommend the **Giant** Lafree Twist

Bus / park & ride

- Public transport is often cheaper than driving, even for two adults and bus lanes are making trips quicker. A professional driver is at least twice as safe as driving yourself, and there is no parking hassle

- Some bus stops have real time displays, or text in the bus stop number to find out when the next bus arrives

- **Traveline** 0871 200 22 33 (national rate) has all National Public Transport information **www.traveline.org.uk**

- Check your Council's bus line or **www.busmap.co.uk** (London) or Doe's Directory **www.barrydoe.plus.com**. **Royal Mail** run rural post bus services.

- **Door to Door** is the site for disabled and less mobile people, or ask Social Services

- People aged 60 or over can get free off-peak bus travel in their local authority or Passenger Transport Executive. Off-peak is after 9.30am Monday to Friday, and all day at weekends.

- In Scotland over 60 year olds and the disabled get free, local and long-distance bus travel. See **Transport Scotland**'s site about Entitlement Cards.

- Freedom Passes give London residents aged 60+ free off peak travel on London's public transport – Tube, buses, trains, Docklands Light Rail (DLR) and trams off peak. 16 and 17 year olds in full time education can get free bus and tram travel in London

If you are unhappy with services write to your operator or **The Bus Appeals Body**.

Bus users breathe a third less pollution than car users.

Trains and underground

Rail travel is statistically very safe and can be faster than a car over long distances or in congested areas.

Don't assume that return journeys are always cheaper – check out the costs of buying two singles instead. Increases on key fares are restricted to match inflation. All discount fares are less than car running costs of 25p a mile (2007).

- Buy tickets in advance and online for better availability of discounts

Looking at the alternatives

- Get 34% off leisure fares and All Zone One Day Travelcards with a Young Persons Railcard (£20 p.a.), plus discounts in participating stores. These are for 16-25 year olds and students attending lessons 15 hours weekly, 20 weeks p.a.

- Get 34% off most fares with a Senior Railcard (£20 p.a.) for 60+ year olds

- Get 33% off 1st and standard fares with a Disabled Railcard (£18)

- Under 11s travelling with an adult get free tube travel.

- Children under 5 years travel free. 5-15 year olds pay half. Adults get 34% off and children 60% off adult fares with a Family Railcard (£20 pa). Up to 4 adults and 4 children qualify if going together.

- **www.railcard.co.uk** details railcards including the SE Network railcard

- Ask for group discounts e.g. **Chiltern Railways'** GroupSave (4 for the price of 2).

- Ask about combined tickets such as **PLUSBUS www.plusbus.info** and taxi pick-up

- There is a Forces Railcard for serving members of the regular forces, their spouses and children. £10 pa for 1/3 off most tickets.

- Smart cards such as London's Oystercard offer prepayment discounts.

- Special needs customers can book in advance for help

- You can reserve space for a non-folding bicycle

- Frequent rail users may want to buy the twice yearly National Rail Timetable, a fares manual or **Travel InfoSystems**' rail or tube planner software

Unlike being caught in a traffic jam, you can claim a refund for a serious train delay. If you are unhappy with services, write to the train operating company. **Passenger Focus** helps those dissatisfied with the response.

See **National Rail Enquiries** 08457 484950 (24 hours), **www.nationalrail.co.uk, www.thetrainline.com, www.transportdirect.info, www.qjump.co.uk, www.traveline.org.uk**, or **www.megatrain.com** value fares.

Coach

Coaches are safe and cost less than standard rail tickets, but can take longer. **National Express** serves over 1,200 UK destinations. See also **Megabus** for journeys between most major UK cities. Current prices (2007):

- Advanced booking Funfares starting at £1 can be booked online.

- 60+ year olds get up to half price discounts on route-sixty fares. No coachcard required

- Up to 30% off with a Young Person's Coachcard. £10

p.a. or £25 for 3 years for full time students and 16-26 year olds.

- Family 2plus2 coach cards (£16 p.a.) enables two children to travel free with two adults. Family 1plus1 (£8 p.a.) enables one child to travel free with an adult.
- Brit Xplorer passes give unlimited travel for 7-28 days from £79.

Coachcards or passes are not valid for trips entirely within Scotland on **Scottish Citylink**.

Hire cars

If you need a car for longer journeys, consider hiring one.

- Look for deals integrating car hire with e.g. rail tickets
- Some firms have loyalty discounts (10% plus) fast track service, and offer a discount if you book online

You can get 55 single days of car hire for less than the fixed costs of owning a small used car.

Car clubs

Car clubs offer access to a choice of vehicles without the hassle and expense of ownership. Cars are parked in designated bays near homes or workplaces and can be booked for as little as an hour by internet or phone. Some clubs have a monthly subscription, others a joining fee. A returnable deposit covers insurance excess fees. Cost per hire involves time used and may include a mileage rate fee.

If you drive less than 6,000 miles p.a., a car club will save you £1000-£1500 a year. Replacing a second car with car club use will bring greater savings.

Other member benefits include:

- A variety of vehicles to suit each particular journey

- No need to pay for tax, insurance or maintenance costs

- Cars are less than 3 years old and have full breakdown cover.

In September 2007 there were 42 car clubs in 37 UK towns and cities, with over 28,000 members using 1,000 cars. **Carplus** have a map and database on their site. See **www.carplus.org.uk** or call 0113 234 9299. Operators include **CityCarClub**, **Whizzgo** and **Streetcar**.

Sharing car ownership

Sharing a car can save £1,000+ per year each for two people. You could set up a car club with friends, neighbours or colleagues, either with a car already owned or by purchasing together. You will need to consider:

- Who will be responsible for servicing, maintenance and insurance

- How you pay for it: e.g. split fixed costs according to time used, and running costs by mileage

───── **SUCCESS STORY** ─────

KW belongs to Leicester's Rusty Car Pool, so called because its first car was an old banger. Now they have 22 members and five or six vehicles, including estates, hatchbacks and a van which converts into a minibus. For KW the group is "mainly about sharing resources because our little terraced streets have too many cars, not everyone needs one and they take the space where kids would have played." A car pool suits those who do not drive everyday and want to share an expensive resource or live on a moderate income. As well as cutting costs and the number of cars on the streets, other pooling benefits are that each vehicle is used more often and efficiently than a private car plus the extra flexibility to use the type of vehicle best suited to the journey's purpose.

- How the car will be booked, where it will be parked

- How to prioritise usage, e.g. whether one person has priority at particular times, certain days of the week, or first come first served. Use car hire as a back up

- A booking system e.g. a diary or wall chart/stickers.

- A system for recording use, e.g. record miles in a logbook. Sharers usually pay for their own petrol, so agree to fill the tank before swapping over, or note petrol costs and miles driven

- Tax issues

- How the sharing arrangement will end if someone decides they want to leave

Carplus publish the Car Club Kit, which is useful for car ownership sharers and car clubs. **Streets Alive** have information on their website and also an advice leaflet about sharing ownership.

Moped, scooter and motorbike

Powered two-wheelers are cheaper to run, easier to park and quicker than cars; they also take up less road space. However, you may have safety concerns. Noise and fumes can be a problem. Road tax increases with engine size.

Alternative fuel scooters are better: the Vectrix Elecric Maxi-Scooter (electric or fuel-cell hybrid), or Intelligent Energy's ENV hydrogen fuel-cell bike. Learner riders must complete a Compulsory Basic Training (CBT) course before riding on the road. Ask the **Driving Standards Agency**.

Other alternatives

Trams, such as the **Stagecoach Supertram** in Sheffield and **Croydon Tramlink** operate in some towns.

Roller blading feels like ice skating. It is quicker than walking, greener and healthier than car use, and does not take much practice. Choose recreational blades (longer than aggressives and with a heel brake) which are faster and harder wearing. Good blades are £85+ (2007).

Skate boarding or using a push scooter is two to three times faster than walking. Boards are very light, and fit easily under your arm or attached to a bag when not in use. Utility skaters need good bearings with big, soft wheels, and should wear protective pads.

Electric scooters can be hired through the **National Federation of Shopmobility UK.**

The **Segway** human transporter is an electric upright machine. A **Trikke** looks like a push scooter in a V-shape. It propels its rider through weight transference between feet.

——— SUCCESS STORY ———

Jemima Jefferson lives in Leytonstone and works in the City of London. She has been riding a motorbike for twenty years.

"If you ride a bike to save time getting to work but you have the mentality of a car driver it isn't long before you break a leg in several places. You must learn riding skills before you venture out into traffic on a bike. It seems that it's almost impossible to learn them when you have been driving a car for a long time – it's a different mind set.

"The beauty of motorbikes is that they are a true alternative – they have a whole lifestyle that goes with them. You can park them all over London on motorcycle parking bays that cost nothing, they are easy to maintain, cheap on fuel and kinder on the environment than cars in queues.

"I like my motorbike – it's fun, quick to get through traffic, exciting on a sunny summer Sunday, and for me, pretty safe. You can't drink and drive if you ride a bike because the risks are too high. The statistics show that old bikers are unlikely to go head first through car windscreens or wrap themselves round trees."

Chapter 4

Changing your travel habits

The psychology of changing

Dawn decisions are crucial! Habit and your first choice of transport influence how you get around for the rest of the day. Think about your first journey of each day and then try changing it for the better. If you are in a hurry, have a lot to carry, or are travelling at night, you may not feel like walking or cycling, so:

- Plan the alternatives for regular first journeys. What type of transport, route, time, who with, etc.?

- Allow time to go by foot or cycle and don't aim to fit in too much, particularly on your first trip

- Get everything you need for your alternative travel ready the night before

- Try to travel in daylight if possible

- Minimise what you carry, particularly on the first trip. Use lockers, delivery or good load-carrying aids

Set yourself targets

1. My car use is .... miles a year. I aim to cut it by ....
% in 6 months, by .... % in a year to under .... miles
p.a.

2. I am usually in a car on .... days a week.
I aim to use a car on only .... days a week by ....
(date).

3. My car's engine capacity is ....cc. I aim to get a smaller
car with a ....cc engine and better fuel efficiency by
.... (date).

4. My household has ...... car(s). I aim reduce it to ...... car(s)
by .... (date).

Check your progress in six and twelve months. Reward
yourself when you reach one of your targets. Then set a
new goal.

Some people deliberately make choosing car travel harder, e.g.:

- Garaging or parking the car at a good walking distance from the door

- Sharing a car or lending it to (insured) drivers to limit availability / temptation

- Hanging up car keys rather than keeping them in a bag

- Deciding not to drive at all on certain days of the week

- Saving up all car-related errands for an allotted day of the week

Stop and think

Ask yourself: "Is the car really necessary?" A car-dependent person will think no further about how to travel – only driving comes to mind. Habits are created by practice, and can be changed! Ask yourself:

- Why am I travelling? What is the purpose?

- Do I really need to travel? If so, how far? Is there a nearer alternative?

- Can I link the trip with another purpose?

- How shall I travel? When is the best time?

- Is there public transport? Can I rearrange to fit timetables?

- Can I share the ride or vehicle costs?

Localise

In Britain, people travel by car for 18% of all trips under 1 mile and for 61% of all trips between 1-2 miles.

Using local goods and services is convenient, saves time, money and the earth's resources, and supports your local economy rather than big business. Make some time for yourself by:

- Using letters, phone, fax, email, text, web, delivery or video conferencing instead of travelling

- Combining journeys by travelling for two or more purposes

— SUCCESS STORY —

When someone wrote off Rosemary Turner's car, she bought a computer with the insurance. This momentous decision opened a more satisfying career as a freelance editor and charity administrator. Rosemary is now true to her values and only does work she approves of. By downshifting "I am free to do the work I love without worrying about over-heads." Rosemary finds walking healthy and meditative. She likes observing the characters on the bus and mixing with different types of people, as she is a writer who otherwise works alone. A taxi helps bring the weekly shop for herself and her daughter up a steep hill.

Chapter 5

Making better use of your car

If you decide to keep your car, what changes can you make to use it less? Can you plan some days without meetings, or use a pool car?

Plan your journeys

In order to analyse your car use, record a personal diary of all car trips for a week. Then see if you can reduce your need to travel, link journeys better, or use your car less. Planning circular trips with more than one stop often cuts overall distance. Try to avoid peak times.

Use a smaller vehicle

Using a smaller car is cheaper, easier to manoeuvre and park and more environmentally friendly.

What type of vehicle?

- What is the car for? What capacity? Try to meet your usual needs, rather than the exceptional journeys

- Light, small cars (e.g. Smart) are more fuel-efficient

- Cars with alternative fuels, save on fuel, VED and congestion charges. See details from the **Energy Saving Trust**'s **Powershift** or see **www.vcacarfueldata.org.uk**

- Cars with low carbon dioxide emissions pay less VED

- Consider buying, hiring or borrowing a boxed roof rack, detachable trailer or large vehicle occasionally

- Tricycles not over 150cc pay just £15 p.a. road tax (2007)

Car purchase criteria

An estimated 20% of a car's total environmental impact is generated in its manufacture – a strong argument for keeping an old car on the road, always assuming it is well maintained.

When buying a car, consider:

- Whole-life costs e.g. price, fuel efficiency, financing (e.g. lease/hire/buy) maintenance, repairs, depreciation and tax

- Total annual cost of use based on your expected annual mileage. See **www.vcacarfueldata.org.uk**

- Fuel consumption figures – similar models of cars vary by over 25%. The average is 7.82 kilometres per litre for a two-wheel drive petrol model. Check fuel consumption and CO_2 emissions at **www.vcacarfueldata.org.uk**

- Insurance and road tax brackets

- Expected reliability

- The NCAP safety class for passengers, pedestrians and cyclists. A highly visible paint colour is safest

- A 'clean' fuel (see page 52) or two fuels. To calculate cost savings from alternative fuels, go to the **Energy Saving Trust** website

See **www.parkers.co.uk** for used car prices.

Use the **National Society for Clean Air**'s free guide *Clean Cars: How to Choose One* or the **ETA**'s Car Buyer's Guide. The **DfT** and **Vehicle Certification Agency** produce figures. **DVLA** have guides on VED rates. See also **www.directgov.co.uk** travel and transport section.

> *40–55 mph is the most economical driving speed. At 70 mph you use up to 30% more fuel than at 50 mph.*

Be safe – slow down

58% of car drivers in Britain routinely break the 30 mph urban limit. Research on three-mile trips across York in stop-go driving conditions found only a 20 second difference between going at 30 and 25 mph.

- Lower speeds are crucial: excessive and inappropriate speed contributes to one third of all crashes. Every one mph less reduces crashes by between 3% and 6%

- Reduce your rural road speed – over 60% of car occupant deaths and 50% of cycle deaths are on rural roads

- Comply with child restraint laws: see **www.childcarseats.org.uk**

> *Consider extra tuition e.g. Pass-Plus or Institute of Advanced Motoring. IAM claim that with their training, crashes are cut by at least 50%. RoSPA also offer driver training.*

Survival and Speed

Vehicle Speed	<10 mph	10–20 mph	20–30 mph	30–40 mph	60 mph
Pedestrian/Cyclist's Survival Chances	very good	95%	55%	15%	almost no chance

- Consider getting eCall fitted. The European Commission want it to be in all new cars by 2009. It notifies emergency services in the event of a crash.

Use energy efficiently

If you change gear between 1,500–2,500 revs per minute you can reduce fuel use by 15% and emissions by 20%.

- Reduce the number of your short trips (under two miles), as a cold car engine produces 60% more fumes and uses more fuel than when warm. Catalytic converters take six or more miles to work

- Use the smallest, lightest vehicle available

- If you need to fit a roof rack, use an aerodynamic box type. An empty roofrack adds 10%+ to fuel bills. Remove a roof rack or trailer when not in use. Load luggage on a roofrack as low a possible, wrapped in plastic sheeting to raise fuel economy by 2%. Try air vents before opening windows, windows before opening sunroofs. Remove any excess weight. Do not fly car flags

- Plan journeys in advance. Start the engine only when ready to go, and set off immediately. Avoid revving up

- Think ahead. Drive lightly and smoothly - heavy feet wear out brake pads and tyres. Aggressive driving increases fuel consumption by over 25%. Pulling away too fast uses 60% more fuel

- Get in the right gear: top is most energy-efficient

- Avoid unnecessary idling (anything over 10 seconds). Switch off to avoid generating more pollution

- Park in the shade to reduce fuel loss due to evaporation

Automatic transmission can add 10-15% to fuel use, and air conditioning uses an average 15% more fuel.

Maintenance

- Check your tyres monthly. Inflating tyres correctly improves safety, lengthens their life and reduce emissions. A 7psi under-inflation wastes half a gallon per tank

- Have your car serviced at least every year, or each 10,000 miles, to ensure the engine is properly tuned. Get the emissions and the catalytic converter checked, as spot checks can be made and fines imposed

- Streamlining kits and aerodynamic styling cut fuel bills

The **Energy Saving Trust** offer free energy packs. The **Vehicle and Operator Services Agency** (VOSA) is the government vehicle inspectorate.

Use cleaner fuels

You could convert your existing car, or buy a cleaner-fuelled car. Alternatives include vehicles running on liquefied petroleum gas (LPG), natural gas, electricity, biofuels (e.g. ethanol and biodiesel) and fuel cells as well as hybrids. 'Clean fuels' can be 50% more fuel efficient than petrol. Diesel is 30% more fuel-efficient than petrol, but has a worse impact on human health. Biodiesel is cleaner than ordinary diesel.

Consider an alternative vehicle

Using an alternative vehicle has the benefit of being cheaper to run than petrol or diesel.

- Hybrid or dual fuel cars can use two fuels, e.g. electric and petrol, like the Toyota Prius or Honda Civic. These can travel up to 60 miles or more on a gallon of petrol. Yet in terms of energy efficiency, a small non-hybrid car such as a Smart car (50-60 mpg) can rival a hybrid and has a lower purchase price

- Gaseous fuels burn cleaner, which reduces piston and cylinder wear and they use less fuel and oil

- Electric vehicles cost just 1p a mile to run/charge up (equivalent to 30-40 pence a gallon)

- Land for biofuels and food crops is in short supply. One study estimates that we would need to convert a quarter of the planet's ground-grown plant matter to biofuels to replace fossil fuels.

- You can save on VED, company car taxes and congestion charges by switching to an alternative fuel

- Fuel cell and lean-burn engines are emerging technologies. For city driving, new compressed air engines are cleanest, and have a range of 120 miles. See **Revolve Global**'s site about the MDI City C.A.T.

For information on the characteristics of alternative fuels see the **Energy Saving Trust** or the **Liquid Petroleum Gas Association, Natural Gas Vehicles Association** or **Electric Vehicles UK, Alternative Vehicles Technology** or **Revolve Global**. The **Energy Saving Trust** lists UK refuelling station sites.

— SUCCESS STORY —

L. Nash and B. Brett from Hereford have two cars but both cycle to work daily and walk to the shops, carrying loads with a trolley. This has cut their driving by about 50 miles a week. They wanted to save money and the "hassle of getting around, as there are very bad jams most days at peak times". Getting rid of their cars is not yet an option as one works as a stonemason and they occasionally move heavy stones and pull trailers. Their advice to others is to find another way of getting to and from work. Benefits are of getting around the locality faster, with less stress and they are fitter. Most importantly, they make "large savings on fuel, spares and depreciation".

Chapter 6

Living without a car

Planning is vital to success. Look at your lifestyle. Is it feasible to give up car ownership completely? Can you travel less, or do things differently? Do you have everything you need to replace your car? If you've decided to take the plunge, here are some tips:

Before you sell your car

- Discuss being car-free with co-owners/your household

- Add up your car costs compared to the alternatives. **www.cuttingyourcaruse.co.uk, www.carclubs.org.uk, www.eta.co.uk** and **www.travelcalculator.org** have a car costs worksheet which does the maths for you

- Begin to try out alternatives and restructure your schedules

- Research and plan how you will make your most frequent journeys. Identify nearest public transport stops, connections and last services, and where to securely park your cycle. Get timetables

Living without a car

- **Traveline** (0871 200 22 33) **www.traveline.org.uk** or **www.transportdirect.info** provides all UK public transport details

- Consider buying a folding bicycle

- Identify the weakest stage or link in your journey and work out how to deal with it

- Work out the easiest walking and cycle routes with low kerbs and gentle gradients. You can plan your route to avoid busy right turns

- Discover your local cycle routes. Information is available from your Council, your local tourist information centre, **Sustrans**, **London Cycling Campaign**, **Stirling Surveys** and **CycleCity Guides**

- Get any maps you might need. Your local **Ordnance Survey** 'Explorer' map will help you to find quiet routes or see **www.cyclemaps.org.uk** or **www.lifecycleuk.org.uk**

- Ring your nearest car hire firm or car club (ask **Carplus**) about occasional hire

- Decide on a date when you will get rid of your car

Online map sources:
www.traveline.org.uk or www.transportdirect.info for all UK public transport links
www.multimap.com or **www.mapquest.com**, or **www.quickmap.com** for London by bus, tube, train or foot
www.busmap.co.uk for London buses
www.thetube.com for London tube

Making it work

The early days will be the most difficult.

- Avoid places where cars predominate i.e. visit local amenities instead of out of town developments

- Keep reminding yourself what you are gaining

- Use the cash you've saved for treats for all involved

- Cash in being car-free by renting out a parking place, drive or garage, or converting a garage into a room for a lodger

- You could consider cutting rent, mortgage or council tax costs by moving somewhere that doesn't have parking

Sharing the load

There are many things you can do to reduce the amount you carry.

- First, rethink your habits. A weekly shop is a car-based concept. Car-free people shop more often

- Use a delivery service, share a car or taxi e.g. for food shopping

- Only take or buy as much as you need and can carry

- Ask others to help, or take loads for you. Offer to pay them

- Leave belongings in left luggage, lockers or lockable cupboard. Storage can also be used for cycling gear

- Hire or borrow a cycle trailer, use a cycle courier, taxi, car or van, and do all your bulky jobs in one go

Weather

Cold, wet or windy weather can be off-putting. So:

- Buy the best modern lightweight, thermal, waterproof and protective clothing that you can afford. Wear layers. You may also need an umbrella and waterproof bag

- Carry or keep spare clothes (e.g. trousers, socks) at work to change into if needed

- Pick sheltered (e.g. tree-lined) routes if possible

- In really bad weather, get a taxi or share a lift

Carrying loads

- Spread weight evenly e.g. use a strong rucksack or back frame with back padding and padded shoulder straps for comfort

- Consider duplicate kit, e.g. two copies of a heavy book or garden tools

- Push or pull a trailer, trolley, handcart, pram, push chair, suitcase on wheels etc.

- On a bike, use panniers, baskets and trailers, or push a bike with loads in a basket, panniers or on both handlebars. Try Bike Bureau by Carradice for a laptop

- A combination of medium-sized rear panniers, medium-sized panniers mounted low on the front and a small handlebar bag is the best way to carry loads on a bike. The heavier the object, the lower it should be

placed for a low centre of gravity. Some front baskets detach to become bags e.g. **Brompton**

- Trailers are available from **Cycle Heaven** and **Bikes and Trailers** among others. **Cycles Maximus** specialise in load-carrying tricycles. Many trailers detach from bikes to become trolleys. Consider using child-carrying trailers for other loads

- If you want to take the dog on a longer journey try a dog cycle trailer, e.g. from **Bikes and Trailers**

Carrying children

- Take public transport and keep the children amused whilst someone else does the driving

- Young children can be carried in cycle trailers, which offer good weather protection and are stable and easy to pull

- On a bike use a child seat or trailer such as one from the Burley range. Some convert into prams e.g. the Transit Delux from **Trek**. **Cycle Heaven** offer mail order

- Older children can pedal with you on a trailer bike, e.g. Mongoose Alleycat from **Kinetics**, or **Bikes and Trailers**

- Tricycles or tandems are good for family cycling. The **CTC** is a source of advice. **Logic Engineering Concepts** manufacture tricycles and cycles for the disabled

- Some school 'escorted walking bus schemes' use a trolley for bags

Chapter 7

Getting active

Things you can do

- If you are employed, discuss Workplace Travel Plans with your employer using the free guide from **Energy Saving Trust**

- Ask your Councillor for car-free hours or days of the week: e.g. parts of Holyrood Park, Edinburgh are car-free on Sundays, and many cities have driving restrictions. Support the **In Town Without My Car** day in September. Ask for a free booklet

- Your school, company or town may already have a car-sharing website. **www.liftshare.com** have links to most

- Parents can ask for a Safe Routes to Schools Project. **Sustrans** or **Living Streets** advise on this

- Join or set up a Cycle Opportunities Group (COG). **Sustrans**, the **CTC** or **Cycle Campaign Network** can advise. Support National **Bike Week** in June

* Transfer your road assistance membership to **ETA**

* Read other inspiring books such as *Car Sick* (see page 96) and *Cycling To Work* (see page 94)

Organisations

There are many organisations aiming to improve transport choices, road safety, the environment, air quality etc. Consider membership and/or joining their email group lists.

- **Campaign for Better Transport** – including Transport Activist Roundtables and Streets for People network. Rapid response egroup

- **Sustrans** – cycling and walking

- **Living Streets** – walking and the street environment

- **Railfuture** – rail services

- **Friends of the Earth** and **Greenpeace** – action on climate change

- **Campaign to Protect Rural England (CPRE)** – country-side protection

- **RoadPeace** and **Brake**– road victim support

- **Driving Standards Agency** – road safety

- **Brake** – road safety

- The **Slower Speeds Initiative** – slower traffic and egroup

- **Royal Society for the Protection of Accidents (RoSPA)** – safety

- **Child Accident Prevention Trust** – safety

- **Children's Play Council** – safety

- **Cyclist's Touring Club (CTC)** – cyclist group
- **National Society for Clean Air**
- **Campaign for Better Transport** – against UK road building
- **Carfree UK** – car-free residential developments
- **Streets Alive** – experts on street party organisation

International websites for activists

www.worldcarfree.net – building the international car-free movement.
www.lesstraffic.com – David Engwicht, traffic reduction author of *Street Reclaiming*.
www.ecoplan.org – Eric Britton on car-free events around the world.
www.carfree.com – J. Crawford, author of *Carfree Cities*.

— SUCCESS STORY —

Analyst programmer Jonathan Powell from Wantage knew he'd never sell his car. But when it was written off ten years ago he didn't replace it. His family of two adults and three children now do 85% fewer car miles. Environmental concerns, saving money and less worry or stress from car journeys were motivating factors. He says he is better off, fitter through cycling and has raised his quality of life as every journey is different. "We occasionally hire newer cars than we could otherwise afford."

Chapter 8

Talking to
your employer

Your manager may be unaware of the various possibilities which can help you to drive less: green travel brings financial and many other benefits to everyone. Ask for a travel plan. For instance, the company will save on having to provide parking, and also demonstrate its environmental credentials.

- Travel and access information, e.g. this book, a leaflet or web page with road, walking and cycling maps, directions, timetables and taxi details. Request Individualised Travel Marketing, where an transport expert analyses trip patterns and suggests changes. It saves around 13% of car trips

- A lift-sharing database or matching scheme, preferential parking and taxi backup

- Car parking restraints such as permits and charges

- Allowances for phone use and walking, cycling, passengers, public transport and taxi use in the course of business

- Home working, flexi-time and compressed working (when you can take a day off provided hours are worked in advance)

CUTTING YOUR CAR USE

- Shifts to fit with public transport

- Cash instead of parking or a company car

- Interest-free travel loans for a bicycle or travel pass. Up to 50% off cycle gear through **BOOOST** or **Cyclescheme**.

- Discounts/subsidies on public transport

- Lockers and showers

- Walking initiatives such as zebra crossings and low kerbs

- Ask for cycle allowances, secure, convenient racks, pool folding bikes, a bike fleet for work/breaks. Some bike shops will hire to companies, and include maintenance contracts. See **www.cyclefriendlyemployers.co.uk**, and *Cycling to Work* (see page 94)

- On-site facilities include snack and drinks machines, picnic tables

- Green traveller breakfasts and lotteries

Get the comprehensive Travel Plan Resources pack for Employers from the **Energy Saving Trust**. When there is a good travel plan, 18% of car drivers change how they travel.

Advice is available from your local travel plan coordinator at most Highway Authorities. Also **Campaign for Better Transport**, **TravelWise**, **Carplus**, **DfT**, **Liftshare.com**, **Association for Commuter Transport**, **ETA**, **Community Transport Association**, **Sustrans**, **Telework Association**. Anna **Semlyen** presents workshops on reducing car use.

Workplace car pools

Many employers offer a pool of cars for business trips. There are other options:

- They could convert this to a car club to make vehicles available to staff for out-of-hours use

- Cars could be run by an independent car club operator with local businesses joining together to make the scheme more viable

- The company could become a corporate member of a car club, and block-book vehicles during business hours with vehicles parked on site

- A small company or self-employed person could register staff with a car club for work and personal use

Workplace car clubs reduce commuting by car for up to 30% of employees. They cut workplace parking pressure and can help ease rush hour traffic.

For more information contact **Carplus**
www.carplus.org.uk

Directory

Airport Express, 30 Eastbourne Terrace, Paddington, London W2 6LE. T0845 6001515 (local) for tickets & update. www.heathrowexpress.com, www.gatwickexpress.com. Trains.

Alternative Technology Association (ATA) see CAT.

Alternative Vehicles Technology (AVT), Blue Lias House, Station Rd, Hatch Beauchamp, Somerset, TA3 6SQ. T01823 480196, F01823 481116. www.avt.uk.com, info@avt.uk.com. Manufacture & convert electric cars.

Anglia Railways see **One** (Greater Anglia).

Arriva plc, www.arriva.co.uk, enquiries@arriva.co.uk. Bus and rail companies in the UK and mainland Europe. UK regional bus companies are: Arriva Midlands, Arriva North East, Arriva North West and Wales, Arriva Scotland West, Arriva the Shires and Essex, Arriva Southern Counties, Arriva Yorkshire. T08701 20 10 88. www.arrivabus.co.uk for bus timetables and information about tickets. Arriva London buses T020 7222 1234; Arriva Trains Wales, St Mary's House, 47 Penarth Road, Cardiff CF10 5DJ. T0845 6061 660. www.arrivatrainswales.co.uk.

Arrive Alive. Highway Code for Young Road Users. See links on www.thinkroadsafety.gov.uk.

Association for Commuter Transport (ACT), 1 Vernon Mews, Vernon St, London W14 0RL. T020 7348 1977, F020 7348 1989. www.act-uk.com mail@act-uk.com. Promotes best practice in travel planning. Comprehensive website including contacts, ACTion newsletters, factsheets, training and events.

A to B Magazine, 40 Manor Road, Dorchester DT1 2AX. T01305 259998, F0870 052 0810. www.atob.org.uk, atob@atob.org.uk. Alternative transport, folding & electric bikes, trailer & public transport magazine. First point of call for car-free and car-light technology.

Automobile Association Ltd (AA), www.theaa.com. Motoring organisation. Motoring costs online calculator and booklet.

A–Z Maps, Fairfield Rd, Borough Green, Sevenoaks, Kent TN15 8PP. T01732 783422. www.a-zmaps.co.uk, shop@a-zmaps.co.uk.

Bicycle Association (BA), to3 The Quadrant, Coventry CV1 2DY. T02476 553838. www.ba-gb.com. office@ba-gb.com. Represents cycle industry.

Bike2Work see **Bike Week**.

Bike For All, www.bikeforall.net. Cyclists' portal, created jointly between the combined cycling industry representative bodies (BA, ACT) and the Department for Transport.

Bike4life, 5 Titian Rd, Hove, BN3 5QR. T01273 729979/07931 570719. www.bikeforlife.org.uk, info@bikeforlife.org.uk. Charity in Brighton & Hove, and working throughout Sussex. Promotes cycling through professional high quality cycle training and events.

Bikebudi.com (from Liftshare). Liftshare is a software company that runs a car share programme for large employers. It has also recently developed a similar programme, called BikeBUDi, where anyone can search for a a cycle companion for their regular commuting journey.

Bikeregister.com, T01689 862708. www.bikeregister.com, www.selecta-mark.co.uk (T01689 860757). Police-preferred product for marking bikes. From £5.95 (2007).

Bikes and Trailers, 49b Cliffe High Street, Lewes, Sussex BN7 2AN. T01273 480479. www.bikesandtrailers.com, info@bikesandtrailers.com. Cycle trailer & trailer bike specialists.

Bike Week, Nick Harvey, Bike Week HQ, 10 South Pallant, Chichester PO19 1SU. T0845 612 0661. www.bikeweek.org.uk, HQ@bikeweek.org.uk. June events supported by green transport organisations. Incorporates Bike2Work.

BOOOST, www.booost.uk.com. Administer tax-efficient way of employees getting up to 50% off the retail price of new bikes and equipment. Payments are made monthly via salary deductions saving both the employer and employee tax. PAYE only – not for the self-employed.

Brake, PO Box 548, Huddersfield HD1 2XZ. T01484 559909 office, BrakeCare Helpline T01484 421611, F01484 559983. www.brake.org.uk, brake@brake.org.uk. Charity for road safety & victims. Organise Road Safety week (September) and Fleet Safety Forum.

British Cycling Federation (BCF), National Cycling Centre, Stuart St, Manchester M11 4DQ. T0870 871 2000, F0870 871 2001. www.british-cycling.org.uk, info@britishcycling.org.uk. Cycle racing, young cyclists & accident help line.

British Human Power Club, www.bhpc.org.uk. Promote innovation & utility in fast, comfy Human Powered Vehicles (HPVs) & recumbent cycles.

British Schools Cycling Association (BSCA), 21 Bedhampton Rd, North End, Portsmouth, Hampshire PO2 7JX. T02392 642226, F02392 660187. www.bsca.org.uk, sue.knight@bsca.org.uk. Train children for leisure and competition cycling, and adults to cycle with children.

British Waterways, Willow Grange, Church Rd, Watford WD17 3QA. T01923 201120. www.waterscape.com, enquiries.hq@britishwater-ways.co.uk. Many towpaths offer safe cycling. Free permits and information.

Bromakin Wheelchairs, 12 Prince William Rd, Loughborough, Leics LE11 5GU. T01509 217569. www.bromakin.co.uk, sales@bromakin.co.uk. Hand-powered recumbent tricycles. Sales and hire.

Brompton Bicycle Ltd, Lionel Rd South, Brentford, Middx TW8 9QR. T020 8232 8484, F020 8232 8181. www.bromptonbicycle.co.uk. Folding bike specialists.

Bus Appeals Body, c/o Bus Users UK, PO Box 2950, Stoke-on-Trent, ST4 9EW. T01782 442855 F01782 442856. www.bususers.org, enquiries@bususers.org. Independent bus complaints review body.

Busmap.co.uk, www.busmap.co.uk. Free London bus map and timetables.

Byways & Bridleways Trust, PO Box 117, Newcastle upon Tyne NE3 5YT. T/F0191 2364086. www.bbtrust.org.uk. Charity for rights of way & countryside access. *Byway & Bridleway* journal.

C2C Rail, FREEPOST ADM3968, Southend SS1 1ZS. T08457 444422 (local rate) for tickets. Customer Relations T0845 601 4873. www.c2crail.co.uk, custrel@c2crail.co.uk. C2C trains link South Essex towns with London Fenchurch Street station.

Campaign for Better Transport (formerly Transport 2000), The Impact Centre, 12–18 Hoxton St, London N1 6NG. T020 7613 0743, F020 7613 5280. info@bettertransport.org.uk, www.bettertransport.org.uk. National environmental transport body campaigning for improved public transport, reduced car dependency and an end to traffic dominance. Works with government, companies and local communities to promote less car use, better facilities for pedestrians and cyclists and a better deal for public transport users. Network of local supporter groups. Publish *Transport Retort* quarterly. Now incorporates Road Block, an alliance against road building.

Campaign to Protect Rural England (CPRE), 128 Southwark St, London SE1 0SW (020 7981 2800 Fax 020 7981 2899. www.cpre.org.uk, info@cpre.org.uk. Charity protecting the countryside, reducing traffic growth. Charter for country lanes & slower speeds. Publish campaigners guides, leaflets, magazine Countryside Voice.

Carboncalculator.com Web-based carbon scoring.

Carfree UK, 29 Heather Park, South Brent, Devon TQ10 9PU. T0117 907 8469. www.carfree.org.uk, info@carfree.org.uk. Promote car-free residential developments in the UK through advice and research.

Carplus – rethinking car use, Suite C17 Joseph's Well, Hanover Walk, Leeds LS3 1AB. T0113 234 9299. www.carplus.org.uk, info@carplus.org.uk. National charity promoting responsible car use. Works with local authorities, developers, employers and community groups towards development of a national network of car clubs and car sharing schemes.

Centre for Alternative Technology (CAT), Machynlleth, Powys SY20 9AZ. T01654 705950, F01654 702782. www.cat.org.uk. Charity with visitor centre, publications, mail order, courses, consultancy & free information on renewable energy, environmental building, energy efficiency, organic growing & alternative sewage systems.

Child Accident Prevention Trust (CAPT), 4th Floor, Cloister Court, 22-26 Farringdon Lane, London, EC1R 3AJ. T020 7608 3828, F020 7608 3674. www.capt.org.uk, safe@capt.org.uk. Charity to prevent, research & evaluate child accidents.

Children's Play Council, 8 Wakley St, London EC1V 7QE. T020 7843 6016. www.ncb.org.uk/cpc, cpc@ncb.org.uk. Promote home zones, safer streets.

Directory

Chiltern Railways, Western House, 14 Rickfords Hill, Aylesbury HP20 2RX. T08456 005 165. www.chilternrailways.co.uk. Trains from Marylebone St to Birmingham Snow Hill, Aylesbury and Kidderminster. Also London to Stratford-upon-Avon.

City Car Club, The Busworks, 39-41 North Road, London N7 9DP. T0845 330 1234, F01484 483 064. www.citycarclub.co.uk, enquiries@citycarclub.co.uk. Largest city car club operator. UK sites in Edinburgh, London, Bath, Bristol, Brighton & Hove, Lichfield, Huddersfield, Poole and Portsmouth.

Community Transport Association, Highbank, Halton Street, Hyde, Cheshire SK14 2NY. T0845 130 6195 for advice service, F0161 351 7221. www.communitytransport.com, advice@ctauk.org. Advice, information & training on running not-for-profit community transport e.g. minibuses. Discounted vehicle purchase. Give advice on blue badges for disabled drivers

Company of Cyclists, Unit 11, Acaster Estate, Cowper Lane, Acaster Malbis, York, YO23 2TX. T01904 778080, F01904 778963. www.companyofcyclists.com, admin@companyofcyclists.com. Cycle road shows, holidays, books. BikeWorks cycling support services for businesses, local authorities, schools and health trusts.

CrossCountry. www.crosscountrytrains.co.uk, info@crosscountrytrains.co.uk. Train operating company replacing Virgin Trains Cross Country, and Central Trains services between Cardiff and Nottingham, and between Birmingham & Stansted Airport.

Croydon Tramlink, Tramlink Info Centre, Unit 5, Suffolk House, George St, Croydon. T020 8681 8300, F0208688 0989. www.tfl.gov.uk/trams.

CTC (Cyclists' Touring Club), Parklands, Railton Rd, Guildford, Surrey GU2 9JX. T0870 873 0060, F0870 873 0064. www.ctc.org.uk, cycling@ctc.org.uk. Working for cycling, mail order bookshop, National Bike Week & Bike to Work Day. Freewheeler Cycle insurance available to non-members. Cycle hire list on website.

Cycle Campaign Network (CCN), 54–57 Allison St, Digbeth, Birmingham B5 5TH. www.cyclenetwork.org.uk, ccn@cyclenetwork.org.uk. Local group details, conferences & CCN News. Free registration to Bicycle User Groups.

CycleCity Guides, The Welsh Mill, Park Hill Drive, Frome, Somerset BA11 2LE. T01373 453533, F01373 452051. www.cyclecityguides.co.uk, info@cyclecityguides.co.uk. Urban cycle map publisher. Database of all UK cycle maps.

Cycle Friendly Employers, www.cyclefriendlyemployers.co.uk. Site by charity Life Cycle UK Bristol.

Cycleguard, Pavilion Insurance Management, Pavilion House, Mercia Business Village, Westwood Business Park Coventry CV4 8HX. T02476 851010, F02476 851080. www.cycleguard.co.uk, sales@cycleguard.co.uk. Third party liability cover. Legal helpline.

Cycle Heaven, 2 Bishopthorpe Rd, York YO23 1JJ. T01904 636578. www.cycle-heaven.co.uk, info@cycle-heaven.co.uk. Alternative transport, cycle trailers for children, folding bikes and Dutch utility bikes.

Cyclescheme Ltd, PO Box 3809, Bath BA1 1WX. T01225 448933. www.cyclescheme.co.uk. Administer tax-efficient way of employees getting up to 50% off the retail price of new bikes and equipment. Payments made monthly via salary deductions, saving both the employer and employee tax. PAYE only – not for the self-employed.

Cycle Training UK Ltd, 83 Lambeth Walk, London SE11 6DX. T020 7582 3535. www.cycletraining.co.uk, info@cycletraining.co.uk. Cycle training and cycle maintenance training in London.

Cycles Maximus, 6–10 Rear of Kensington Place, London Rd, Bath BA1 6AW. T01225 319414, F01225 446055. www.cyclesmaximus.com info@cyclesmaximus.com. Pedicab, Rickshaws and Cargo Trikes: zero pollution transport solutions.

Datatag ID Ltd, T01932 358100, F01932 358139. www.datatag.co.uk, info@datatag.co.uk. Electronic tagging system.

Department for Education & Skills (DfES) Publications T0845 602 2260 (local). www.dfes.gov.uk, dfes@prolog.uk.com. Free guides including *A Safer Journey to School*.

Department for Transport (DfT), 3/34 Great Minster House, 76 Marsham St, London SW1P 4DR Enquiry Helpdesk T020 7944 8300. Free Literature, PO Box 236, Wetherby, West Yorks, LS23 7NB (0870 122 6236 (national). www.dft.gov.uk, dft@twoten.press.net. Charging & Local Transport Division T020 7944 2478 for free Traffic Advisory Leaflets. Travel Awareness T020 7944 4094.

Docklands Light Railway see **Transport for London**

Doe's Directory of Bus & Rail Timetables, websites and Enquiry Offices, www.barrydoe.plus.com.

Door to Door, www.dptac.gov.uk/door-to-door. Government site compiled by TRIPSCOPE for those with mobility problems.

Driving Standards Agency (DSA), Customer Services T0115 901 2500. www.dsa.gov.uk, publications.dsa@safedriving.org.uk. DSA contributes to the road safety of drivers, riders and all other road users. Safe Driving for Life skills books. www.ask-what-if.com boosts awareness of hazards and ability to avoid accidents. www.arrivealive.info advises young people about the driving test & offers free talks. Pass Plus courses for new drivers.

Driver & Vehicle Licensing Agency (DVLA), Swansea SA6 7JL. T0870 240 0009 (premium). www.dvla.gov.uk. Maintains registers of drivers and vehicles. Collects vehicle excise duty (VED or car tax).

East Midlands Trains. T020 7620 5159. www.eastmidlandstrains.co.uk, getintouch@eastmidlandstrains.co.uk Train operating company. Midland Mainline, and Central Trains from Derby , Nottingham & Lincoln from Nov 2007

Ecoplan, www.ecoplan.org. The Commons: open society sustainability initiative. Problem-solving site on sustainable transport. Active egroup.

Electric Vehicles UK www.evuk.co.uk Electric vehicles site and archive of Electric Vehicles Association. Campaign for long-range electric vehicles.

Energy Saving Trust, 21 Dartmouth St, London SW1H 9BP. T0845 602 1425 (local), F020 7654 2460. www.est.org.uk. Promote cleaner, lower-carbon vehicles and fuels, eco-friendly driving techniques and low-carbon transport alternatives. Advise organisations on fleet efficiency or workplace travel planning. Advise individuals on cutting emissions. Alternative fuel vehicle refuelling infrastructure list. Powershift register of cars, which when converted to LPG, are exempt from the Congestion Charge.

Environmental Transport Association (ETA), 68 High St, Weybridge KT13 8RS. T0800 212 810. www.eta.co.uk, eta@eta.co.uk. Ethical breakdown & cycling assistance, insurance. Organise Green Transport Week. Owned by a charity.

Eurostar Group Ltd www.eurostar.com, info@eurostar.com. High-speed rail service directly linking the UK to France and Belgium via the Channel Tunnel. Runs from Waterloo until 13 Nov 2007, then from St Pancras.

First Capital Connect, Freepost RRBR-REEJ-KTKY, Customer Relations Department, PO Box 443, Plymouth PL4 6WP. T0845 0264700, F0845 6769904. www.firstcapitalconnect.co.uk. Operate Thameslink and Great Northern rail franchises. Cross-London rail services from Bedford through to Brighton and to Luton and Gatwick Airports.

First Great Western Trains, Freepost SWB40576, Plymouth PL4 6ZZ. T08457 48 49 50 for rail enquiries, T08457 000 125 for tickets. www.firstgreatwestern.co.uk. Trains across the south and west of England on the former Wessex Trains, First Great Western Link and First Great Western routes.

First Group, T08457 000 125. Transport operators.

First ScotRail, Atrium Court, 50 Waterloo Street, Glasgow G2 6HQ. T08700 005151 www.firstscotrail.com. Rail operating company for Scotland.

Forestry Commission, T0845 3673787. www.forestry.gov.uk. Cycle access woodland maps.

Friends of the Earth, 26–28 Underwood St, London N1 7JQ. T020 7490 1555. www.foe.co.uk, info@foe.co.uk. Campaigning organisation to protect & improve conditions for life on Earth now and for the future. Publish *Earthmatters* magazine.

Gatwick Express, 52 Grosvenor Gdns, London SW1W 0AU. T020 7973 5000. www.gatwickexpress.co.uk. Regular trains between Central London and Gatwick Airport. Run by National Express.

Giant (UK) Ltd, 1st Floor, Boland House, Nottingham Industrial Estate, Ruddington Lane, Wilford, Nottingham, NG11 7EP. T0115 977 5900. www.giant-bicycle.com, info@giant-bicycles.co.uk. Cycle manufacturer.

Global Action Plan UK, 8 Fulwood Place, London WC1V 6HG. T020 7405 5633, F020 7831 6244. www.globalactionplan.org.uk, all@global-actionplan.org.uk. Range of practical action based programmes for sustainability. Site includes green score and carbon calculator.

GNER, Main HQ, Station Rd, York YO1 6HT. T08457 225 225 (local rate) tickets & update daily. www.gner.co.uk. Rail services on the East Coast Main Line between London King's Cross, the East Midlands, Yorkshire, the North East of England and Scotland. 10% discount online. GNER train franchise for the East Coast main line will be taken over by **National Express East Coast** in December 2007.

Green Books, Foxhole, Dartington, Totnes, Devon TQ9 6EB. T01803 863260, F01803 863843. www.greenbooks.co.uk, sales@greenbooks.co.uk. The publishers of this book and others on environmental & social issues including organics, eco-building & eco-politics.

Green Score, www.greenscore.org.uk, Environmental calculator from Global Action Plan.

Greenpeace, Canonbury Villas, London N1 2PN. T020 7865 8100. www.greenpeace.org.uk, info@uk.greenpeace.org. Non-violent action on climate change & energy.

GT Bicycles www.gtbicycles.com. Bikes.

Heathrow Connect, Freepost RLRZ-TZXE-BYKY, 3rd Floor, 30 Eastbourne Terrace, London W2 6LE. T0845 678 6975 www.heathrow-connect.com queries@heathrowconnect.com. Trains from London Paddington to Heathrow airport.

Hedgehogs, www.hedgehogs.gov.uk. Road safety site for children.

HOP Associates, 55 West St, Comberton, Cambridge CB3 7DS. T01223 264485, F020 7570 0820. www.hop.co.uk. Information & communication consultants, mainly to firms. Promote sustainable work & travel behaviour. Research travel substitution and virtual-mobility.

Hull Trains, Premier House, Ferensway, Hull, HU1 3UF. T0845 676 9905. www.hulltrains.co.uk, customer.services@hulltrains.co.uk. Kings Cross to Hull.

Institute of Advanced Motorists, IAM House, 510 Chiswick High Rd, London W4 5RG. T020 8996 9600, F020 8996 9601. www.iam.org.uk. Charity to develop advanced driving and motorcycle riding skills for road safety.

CUTTING YOUR CAR USE

In Town without my Car! T020 8946 0912. www.itwmc.gov.uk, richard.m.evans@ntlworld.com. Coordinating car-free awareness & events for 22 September. Active egroup. For a free Good Practice Guide contact DfT Free Literature, T0870 1226 236. dft@twoten.press.net. Product code: 67 RRLG 02612.

Island Line, St Johns Rd Station, Ryde, Isle of Wight PO33 2BA. T08457 484950. www.island-line.co.uk. Trains operated by Stagecoach Group.

Kinetics, 0141 942 2552. www.kinetics-online.co.uk, mail@kinetics-online.co.uk. Electric bikes, scooters, folding and trailer bikes.

Life Cycle UK, 86 Colston Street, Bristol BS1 5BB. T0117 929 0440, F0117 927 7774. www.lifecycleuk.org.uk, post@lifecycleuk.org.uk. Aims to inspire people and to equip with skills, knowledge and confidence to make cycling part of their everyday lives. Cycle training, events, provides literature, conferences and seminars

Liftshare, Butterfly Hall, Attleborough, Norfolk, NR17 1AB. T08700 780225, Call Centre T08700 11 11 99. www.liftshare.com, info@lift-share.com. UK's integrated car sharing scheme specialists. Car share, car park management and public transport information web services to communities, businesses and individuals. Framework for the national network of regional schemes.

Liquid Petroleum Gas Association, Pavilion 16, Headlands Business Park, Salisbury Road, Ringwood, Hampshire BH24 3PB. www.lpga.co.uk, mail@lpga.co.uk. Non-profit organisation supporting members (LPG companies) through the promotion of the benefits of LPG (principally propane and butane) and of safe operations and standards.

Living Streets (formerly Pedestrians Association) / Walk to School, 31–33 Bondway, London SW8 1SJ. T020 7820 1010, F020 7820 8208. www.livingstreets.org.uk, info@livingstreets.org.uk. Charity to protect and promote the rights of walkers and the benefits of walking. Publish *Living Streets* and *Walk to School* magazines. www.walktoschool.org.uk. Free info with A5 SAE.

Logic Engineering Concepts Ltd, Nash Works, Nash Lane Belbroughton nr. Stourbridge DY9 9TD. T01562 731 355. www.cyclemakers.com. Manufacture tricycles and products for the disabled. Off the shelf and custom-built cycles and accessories.

Directory

London Cycling Campaign, 2 Newham's Row, off Bermondsey Street, London SE1 3UZ. T020 7234 9310, F020 7234 9319. www.lcc.org.uk, office@lcc.org.uk. LCC works to make London a world-class cycling city. It provides services for and campaigns on behalf of over 10,000 individual and corporate members.

London Midland. www.londonmidland.co.uk. Train operating company of the West Midlands franchise replacing Silverlink County, and Central Trains services around Birmingham from Nov 2007.

London Overground. www.tfl.gov.uk. Train operating company reeplacing Silverlink Metro from Nov 2007.

London Recumbents, Rangers Yard, Dulwich Pk, College Road, London SE21 7BQ. T020 8299 6636. www.londonrecumbents.com, recumbents@aol.com. Also at Staff Yard, Battersea Park, London SW11 4NJ. T020 7498 6543. Recumbent bikes.

London TravelWatch, 6 Middle Street London EC1A 7JA. T020 7505 9000, F020 7505 9003. www.LondonTravelwatch.org.uk, enquiries@londontravelwatch.org.uk. Independent watchdog body dealing with customer complaints regarding Transport for London.

Mapquest.com, www.mapquest.com. Interactive on-line atlas and street plan. T0845 6000 650 (opening hours 6am to 10pm).

Megabus.com Low cost no-frills intercity bus service, offering tickets fom London to Glasgow.

Megatrain.com, T0901 331 0031. Low cost intercity train fares from South West Trains and Virgin Trains through Stagecoach Group.

Merseyrail Electrics (tickets through National Rail Enquiries) Customer services T0151 702 2071. www.merseyrail.org.

Midland Mainline, Midland House Nelson St Derby, East Midlands, DE1 2SA. T08457 125 678 (local) Mon-Fri 0800–1800, F01332 263895, Textphone 08457 078 051. www.midlandmainline.com, feedback@midlandmainline.com. Trains between Yorkshire, the East Midlands and London St Pancras. Franchise goes to **East Midlands Trains** after Nov 2007.

Moteur Development International (MDI), www.theaircar.com. Compressed air engines with a range of 120 miles. MDI city C.A.T. not yet in production.

Multimap.com, www.multimap.com. Free internet street maps and door to door travel directions, weather forecasts. Links to location information such as hotels.

National Byway (The), PO Box 128 Newark Notts NG23 6BL. T01636 636818. www.thenationalbyway.org, enquiries@thenationalbyway.org. Britain's heritage cycling 4,000-mile route.

National Cabline, 0800 123444. Calls route to a local taxi firm member based on STD code of phone used.

National CarShare, 8 Cressida Chase, Warfield, Bracknell, Berkshire, RG42 3UD. T01344 861600. www.nationalcarshare.co.uk, contact@nationalcarshare.co.uk. Car share information service. Interactive voice response line. Members dial 01344 648250 from any touch-tone telephone, enter their membership number and PIN and then listen to options.

National Cycling Training Helpline T0870 607 0415.

National Express Ltd, Ensign Court, 4 Vicarage Rd, Edgbaston, Birmingham B15 3ES. T08705 808080 (national) 08.00–20.00, 2–3 days by post. Disabled helpline 0121 423 8479. Textphone 0121 455 0086. www.nationalexpress.com, customerrelations@nationalexpress.co.uk. Coaches to 1,200+ UK destinations and Eurolines. Train services include C2C, Central Trains, Gatwick Express, Midland Mainline, One, Silverlink and Stanstead Express. Coach tickets can now be emailed

National Express East Coast. www.youreastcoast.co.uk. Train operating company replacing GNER from Dec 2007.

National Federation of Shopmobility (NFSUK), Enham Place, Enham Alamein, Andover, Hants, SP11 6JS. T08456 442 446, F08456 444 442. www.justmobility.com/shop, info@shopmobilityuk.org. Charity to advise and support new and existing shopmobility schemes of electric scooter loans.

National Rail Enquiries UK, T08457 484950 (local rate). www.national-rail.co.uk. Timetable from stations and newsagents.

National Society for Clean Air and Environmental Protection (NSCA), 44 Grand Parade, Brighton BN2 9QA. T01273 878770, F01273 606626. www.nsca.org.uk, admin@nsca.org.uk. Charity for the reduction of environmental pollution e.g. noise and air quality.

Nationwide Cycle Registration, 8 Highridge Road, Bishopsworth, Bristol BS13 8HA. T0117 964 2187. www.thencr.co.uk, enquiries@thencr.co.uk. Cycle database and internet publishing of details of lost bikes. £5.95 one-off fee (2007).

Natural Gas Vehicle Association (NGVA), 36 Holly Walk, Leamington Spa, Warwickshire, CV32 4LY. T01926 462900, F01926 462919. www.ngva.co.uk, info@ngva.co.uk. UK's trade association for developers of vehicles powered by compressed natural gas (CNG).

Network Rail, 40 Melton Street, London NW1 2EE. T020 7557 8000, F020 7557 9000. www.networkrail.co.uk. Owns and operates Britain's rail infrastructure.

NI Railways and Translink Timetable enquiries T028 90 666630. www.nirailways.co.uk. Northern Ireland rail and Ulsterbus operators.

Northern Ireland Road Service. www.roadsni.gov.uk Build and maintain roads.

Northern Rail, Northern House, 9 Rougier Street, York, YO1 6HZ. T0845 00 00 125. www.northernrail.org, customer.relations@northern-rail.org. Rail operating company serving Northern England.

one Railway, Floor One, Oliver's Yard, 55 City Road, London, EC1Y 1HQ. T0845 600 7245. www.onerailway.com. Train operator providing services to London Liverpool Street and the East of England.

Ordnance Survey (OS), Romsey Road, Maybush, Southampton SO16 4GU. T08456 050505 (local rate), F023 8079 2615. www.ordnancesurvey.co.uk, customerservices@ordnancesurvey.co.uk. Britain's national mapping agency.

Parkers, www.parkers.co.uk. Used car prices.

Passenger Focus, Freepost W1521, Warrington WA4 6GP. T08453 022 022.www.passengerfocus.org.uk, hello@passengerfocus.org.uk. Independent rail consumer watchdog.

PASS PLUS, Driving Standards Agency, Stanley House, 56 Talbot Street Nottingham, NG1 5GU. T0115 901 2633. www.passplus.org.uk, PassPlus@dsa.gsi.gov.uk. Training scheme by the Driving Standards Agency for newly qualified drivers for safety & to save on insurance premiums. Website lists councils offering discounts.

Permaculture Magazine, The Sustainability Centre, East Meon, Hants GU32 1HR. T0845 458 4150 (local rate) or 01730 823311, F01730 823322. www.permaculture.co.uk, info@permaculture.co.uk. Over 500 books, videos, products and tools for sustainable living.

PLUSBUS. www.plusbus.info. Unlimited bus travel with your rail ticket from £2 per day.

Pure Biodiesel Ltd, www.purebiodiesel.co.uk. Lists British biodiesel outlets.

Q Jump, www.qjump.co.uk. Online rail ticket site.

RAC, T08705 722 722 (freephone). Breakdown services T0800 731 7090, Traffic information 1740 from a mobile phone, T0906 470 1740 from a landline. www.rac.co.uk. Free internet route planner.

Rail enquiries – see National Rail Enquiries or www.nationalrail.co.uk.

Railfuture, www.railfuture.org.uk, info@railfuture.org.uk. Voluntary, independent organisation campaigning for better rail services for passengers and freight.

Rail Passengers Council see **Passenger Focus**.

Ramblers Association, 2nd Floor, Camelford House, 87–90 Albert Embankment, London SE1 7TW. T020 7339 8500, F020 7339 8501. www.ramblers.org.uk, ramblers@ramblers.org.uk. Campaign for rights of way, local walking groups.

Re-Cycle, Unit A, Global Park, Moorside, Eastgates, Colchester Essex CO1 2TW. T0845 458 0852 (local) or 01206 863111. www.re-cycle.org, info@re-cycle.org. Charity relieving poverty by taking second-hand bikes and parts to Africa. Collection hubs around UK.

Revolve Global Ltd, 101 Hornsey Lane, London, N6 5LW. T07711 99 41 60. info@revolve.ws, www.revolve.ws. UK's leading organisation championing emissions-reductions and solutions to combat global warming in vehicles, with an emphasis on hydrogen and fuel-cell powered mobility.

Road Block is now a project of the **Campaign for Better Transport**.

RoadPeace, PO Box 2579, London NW10 3PW. Helpline T0845 4500 355, office T020 8838 5102, F020 8838 5103. www.roadpeace.org, info@roadpeace.org. Charity supporting those bereaved or injured in a road crash. Working for road safety. Reports, newsletters & *Safety First* magazine.

Directory

Royal Mail. www.royalmail.com. Mail and post bus services.

Royal Society for the Prevention of Accidents (RoSPA), Edgbaston Park, 353 Bristol Rd, Edgbaston, Birmingham B5 7ST. T0121 248 2000, F0121 248 2001. www.rospa.co.uk, help@rospa.com. Safety charity & training: Advanced Driving Test & Diplomas in Advanced Driving & Riding Motorcycles.

Safe Routes to Schools, www.saferoutestoschools.org.uk. Sustrans site combining Walk to School and Bike it schemes.

Scottish City Link, Customer Services, Buchanan Bus Station, Killermont Street, Glasgow G2 3NP. T08705 505050 (1 day by post), F0141 332 4488. www.citylink.co.uk, info@citylink.co.uk. Coaches to 200 Scottish destinations.

Segway-UK, 43 Bakewell Rd, Matlock, Derbyshire DE4 3AU. T01629 56666, F01629 57777. info@segway-uk.net, www.segway-uk.net. The Segway Human Transporter (HT) is a two-wheeled, self-balancing, electric transportation device with dynamic stabilization.

Semlyen, Anna, 24 Grange Street, York Y010 4BH. T01904 654355. www.cuttingyourcaruse.co.uk, info@cuttingyourcaruse.co.uk. Author, traffic reduction consultant & speaker.

Shareajourney.com Ltd, Kesteven Business Centre, 2 Kesteven Street, Sleaford, Lincolnshire NG34 7DT. www.shareajourney.com. Individuals: enquiries@shareajourney.com Corporate: corporate@shareajourney.com. Web lift-share matching service.

Silverlink Trains, 10th Floor, 207 Old Street, London EC1V 9NR. Silverlink County T0845 601 4868, Metro T0845 601 4867. www.silver-link-trains.com. Silverlink County operates between London and Northampton until Nov 2007, when it is replaced by **London Midland**. Silverlink Metro operates through North, East and West London until Nov 2007, when it is replaced by **London Overground**. Silverlink Metro operates through North, East and West London. Run by National Express.

Slower Speeds Initiative (SSI), PO Box 19, Hereford HR1 1XJ. T0845 345 8459. www.slower-speeds.org.uk, info@slower-speeds.org.uk. Road safety charity & campaign coalition, cutting carbon emmisions, active egroup.

Smart Moves Ltd see **CityCarClub**.

Society of Motor Manufacturers & Traders (SMMT), Customer Relations, Forbes House, Halkin Street, London SW1X 7DS. T020 7235 7000, F020 7235 7112. www.smmt.co.uk, communications@smmt.co.uk. Complaints about cars under manufacturer's warranty.

Soil Association, Bristol House, 40–56 Victoria St, Bristol BS1 6BY. T0117 314 5000, F0117 314 5001. www.soilassociation.org, www.whyorganic.org, info@soilassociation.org. Charity for organic food and farming. Local food links pack.

Southeastern Trains, PO Box 286, Plymouth, PL4 6WU. T0845 000 2222. www.southeasternrailway.co.uk. Serves Kent, South-East London and East Essex.

Southern Railways, T08451 27 29 20. www.southernrailway.com. Trains for the south London Metro area, London to Brighton, plus the south coast.

South West Trains, Friars Bridge Court, 41-45 Blackfriars Road, London SE1 8NZ. T08700 00 5151. www.southwesttrains.co.uk. Trains operated by Stagecoach Group.

Stagecoach Group, www.stagecoach.com. Operate coaches, buses, trains and trams.

Stagecoach Supertram Sheffield, Nunnery Depot, Woodbourne Road, Sheffield S9 3LS. T0114 272 8282. www.supertram.com enquiries@supertram.com. Trams.

Stanfords, 12–14 Long Acre, London WC2E 9LP. T020 7836 1321, F020 7836 0189. www.stanfords.co.uk. sales@stanfords.co.uk. Maps.

Stansted Express, 1, Grosvenor House 112-114 Prince of Wales Road, Norwich NR1 1NS. T0845 600 7245. www.standstedexpress.co.uk, customer.services@onerailway.com. Trains between Central London and Stansted Airport.

Stationery Office (The), TSO Orders/Post Cash Dept, PO Box 29, Norwich NR3 1GN. T0870 600 5522. www.tso.co.uk. customer.services@tso.co.uk. The Highway Code, Planning Policy Guidance Notes and government publications. Online bookstore.

Stirling Surveys, Unit 87, Stirling Enterprise Park, Stirling FK7 7RP. T01786 479866, F01786 472914. www.stirlingsurveys.co.uk, info@stirlingsurveys.co.uk. Footprint (www.footprintmaps.co.uk) & cycle maps.

Directory

Streetcar, Park House, 8 Lombard Road, Wimbledon, SW19 3TZ. T0845 644 8475. www.streetcar.co.uk, services@streetcar.co.uk. Pay-as-you-go-car club in London, Brighton & Southampton.

Streetmap, www.streetmap.co.uk. Web maps.

Streets Alive Ltd, 86 Colston Street, Bristol BS1 5BB. T0117 922 5708. www.streetsalive.net, www.streetparty.org.uk. Promoting culture through traffic-free street events. Began in Bristol, going national. Leaflet on car ownership sharing.

Sustrans, PO Box 21, Bristol BS99 2HA. Info T0845 113 0065, T0117 926 8893, F0117 929 4173. www.sustrans.org.uk, info@sustrans.org.uk. Practical charity for walking & cycling. National Cycle Network, Safe Routes to Schools, free catalogue of maps & technical publications. Free Safe Routes video. Map sales T0845 116 0065.

Tandem Club, www.tandem-club.org.uk, secretary@tandem-club.org.uk. Magazine & handbook, cycling club rides.

Technicolour Tyre Co, PO Box 373, Brookwood, Woking, Surrey GU24 0BA T01483 797675 F01483 797681. Mail order safety reflectives.

Telework Association T0800 616008 (freephone) www.telework.org.uk, enquiries@telework.org.uk. Not-for-profit organisation for flexible working. Teleworker magazine and handbook.

THINK! Road Safety, www.thinkroadsafety.gov.uk. DfT website. Links to Hedgehogs and Arrive Alive Highway Code for Young Road Users.

Thomas Cook, T0870 750 5711. www.thomascook.com. Rail maps & European timetable.

Train Line, www.thetrainline.com. Enquiries and bookings.

Traintaxi, www.traintaxi.co.uk. Guide to taxis serving all train, tram, metro and underground stations in Great Britain.

TRANSform Scotland, Lamb's House, Burgess Street, Edinburgh EH6 6RD. T0131 467 7714, F0131 554 8656. www.transformscotland.org.uk, info@transformscotland.org.uk. Non-profit campaign for sustainable transport in Scotland.

TransPennine Express, ADMAIL 3878, FREEPOST Manchester M1 9YB. T0845 678 6974. www.tpexpress.co.uk. Customer Relations T0845 6001671, F0845 6008363. Trains across the North of England.

Transport 2000 see **Campaign for Better Transport**

CUTTING YOUR CAR USE

Transport Direct, www.transportdirect.info. Britain's free online journey planner. Door-to-door and postcode planner, maps and live travel details.

Transport for All, Units 1 and 2, 336 Brixton Road, London SW9 7AA. T0207 7372339. www.transportforall.com, contactus@transportforall.com. London-based campaign for accessible transport for disabled & older people.

Transport for London (TfL), Customer Services, 23rd Floor Empress State Building, Empress Approach, London SW6 1TR. www.tfl.gov.uk. London Travel Info T020 7222 1234, London Buses T0845 300 7000, Travelcheck T020 7222 1200, Oyster helpline T0845 330 9876. Customer relations T020 7222 5600. Congestion charges www.cclondon.com, T0845 900 1234. Tube www.thetube.com. Bus & river buses. Real time travel info & journey plans, free walking maps.

Transport Scotland, Buchanan House, 58 Port Dundas Rd, Glasgow G4 0HF. T0141 272 7170. www.transportscotland.gov.uk, freebus@transportscotland.gsi.gov.uk. National Entitlement cards for free senior and disabled bus travel in Scotland. Young persons scheme to follow.

Traveline T0871 200 22 33 (national rate) 08.00–20.00 daily. www.traveline.org.uk. National travel information.

Travel InfoSystems, Suite 1, Grand Union House, 20 Kentish Town Rd, London, NW1 9NX. T020 7428 1288. www.travelinfosystems.com, enquiries@travelinfosystems.com. Rail route planning software, TubePlanner.

TravelWise Association (NTWA), T01273 272936. www.travelwise.org.uk, editor@travelwise.org.uk. Campaign to change attitudes to car use.

TravelWise Northern Ireland, Campaign Office, Clarence Court, 10–18 Adelaide Street, Belfast BT2 8GB. Travelwise NI Information Line T0845 378 0908. www.travelwiseni.com. Promoting sustainable transport options.

Trek. T01908 282626. www.trekbike.co.uk. Cycles & trailers.

Trikke UK. 0845 450 7278. www.trikkeuk.com, info@trikkeuk.com. Trikke three-wheeled cambering vehicles are human-powered machines to allow a rider to propel a chainless, pedal-less device forward without ever touching foot to ground.

A–Z Guide

Vehicle Certification Agency (VCA), The Eastgate Office Centre, Eastgate Rd, Bristol BS5 6XX. T0117 951 5151. www.vca.gov.uk, enquiries@vca.gov.uk. Car fuel consumption and carbon emissions figures. www.vcacarfueldata.org.uk lists cars with alternative fuels.

Vehicle & Operator Services Agency (VOSA) T0870 6060440, MOT enquiry T0870 3300444, www.vosa.gov.uk. Executive Agency of the DfT.

Velo Vision Magazine, York Environmental Centre, St. Nicholas Fields, Bull Lane, York YO10 3EN. T/F01904 438224. www.velovision.com, peter@velovision.com. Magazine about transport bikes and products. Recumbents a speciality.

Virgin Trains, T08457 222 333 (local rate) tickets. www.virgintrains.co.uk, www.thetrainline.com, www.megatrain.com, www.virgin.com/trains is trialling print-at-home tickets. Assistance T08457 443366 (local) with 24 hrs notice. Group travel T0870 010 4490. Runs CrossCountry (until Nov 2007) and West Coast train routes.

Virtual Mobility Knowledge Base, www.virtual-mobility.com. Information and Communications technologies (ICT) as an alternative to physical mobility. Results of a project commissioned by the UK Department of Transport. Extensive database on e-work (telework, telecommuting), e-business & e-commerce and e-services (e-government services, e-learning, telemedicine, etc).

Walk to School, www.walktoschool.org.uk. Campaign by TravelWise and Living Streets.

WhizzGo Ltd, Emco House, 5-7 New York Rd, Leeds LS2 7PJ. T0870 446 6000. www.whizzgo.co.uk, contact@whizzgo.co.uk. Car club operator, the viable way to stop owning a car in Leeds, London, Brighton, Southampton, Liverpool and York.

Workbike.org Human-powered transport site. Lists manufacturers of bikes, trikes, quads, trailers and pedicabs. Lists perators of human powered cargo and pedicab services.

World Carfree Network, Kratka26, 100 00 Prague 10, Czech Republic. www.worldcarfree.net, info@worldcarfree.net. Building & maintaining the global carfree movement. *Car Busters* magazine (£20 p.a., 2007), Carfree Green Pages directory, conferences, resources, email news, autoholics anonymous campaign.

Distance, speed and fuel conversion tables

Distance
1 yard = 91.4 centimetres   1 metre = 3.279 feet
1 kilometre = 1090 yards or 0.6213 miles
1 mile = 1760 yards or 1.6093 kilometres

Speed

mph	10	20	30	40	50	60	70
kmph	16	32	48	64	80	96	112

Fuel Consumption
1 gallon = 4.546 litres

miles per gallon	10	15	20	25	30	35	40	45	50
miles per litre	2.2	3.3	4.4	5.5	6.6	7.7	8.8	9.9	11

Feedback

Feedback is *very welcome*. Please let us know of other organisations you think should be in the directory, new addresses or about services or products which help to cut car use.

info@cuttingyourcaruse.co.uk
www.cuttingyourcaruse.co.uk
Anna Semlyen, c/o Green Books,
Foxhole, Dartington, Totnes, Devon TQ9 6EB, UK.

About the Author

Anna Semlyen is car-free by choice and organises her life so that her main activities are close to where she lives. She walks, pushes a pram and rides a Gazelle upright bike with a Chariot child trailer or U plus 2 trailer bike. Anna shares lifts and takes taxis, buses and trains.

Anna runs Cutting Your Car Use consultancy services, which include workshops on reducing car use — see www.cuttingyourcaruse.co.uk.

She is the 'agony aunt' advice columnist in *Car Busters* magazine for the **World Carfree Network**, and has written for *Transport Retort*, *Green World*, *A to B*, *Bycycle* and *Fleet Operator* magazines.

Anna is a single mum who enjoys teaching yoga and juggling. She writes poetry and dances salsa. She campaigns for children's spaces and outdoor play. This is her second book.

ustrans national
cycle network

Index

Index

Also in the Green Books Guides series:

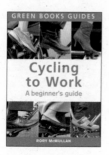

Cycling to Work
by Rory McMullan
Gives support and encouragement to
get to work by bike.
£4.95 paperback

Greening Your Office
by Jon Clift and Amanda Cuthbert
Packed with ideas for making your
workplace eco-friendly.
£4.95 paperback

Reduce, Reuse, Recycle
by Nicky Scott
Includes an A–Z guide for household
recycling. £4.95 paperback

Also in the Green Books Guides series:

Composting: an easy household guide
by Nicky Scott

Tells you everything you need to know for successful home composting.
£4.95 paperback

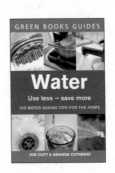

Water: use less – save more
by Jon Clift and Amanda Cuthbert

100 water-saving tips for the home.
£4.95 paperback

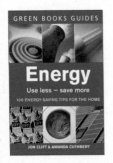

Energy: use less – save more
by Jon Clift and Amanda Cuthbert

100 energy-saving tips for the home.
£4.95 paperback

Also available from Green Books:

Car Sick
by Lynn Sloman
A passionate, well-argued case for
moving away from a car-centred to
a people-centred society.
£10.95 paperback

For our complete book list, see our website:
www.greenbooks.co.uk